William Golding

by SAMUEL HYNES

SECOND EDITION

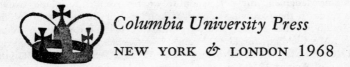

Columbia University Press
NEW YORK & LONDON 1968

COLUMBIA ESSAYS ON MODERN WRITERS is a series of critical studies of English, Continental, and other writers whose works are of contemporary artistic and intellectual significance.

Editor: William York Tindall

Advisory Editors

Jacques Barzun   W. T. H. Jackson   Joseph A. Mazzeo   Justin O'Brien

William Golding is Number 2 of the series.

SAMUEL HYNES is Professor of English at Northwestern University. He is the author of *The Pattern of Hardy's Poetry* and *The Edwardian Turn of Mind* and editor of *Further Speculations by T. E. Hulme* and *The Author's Craft and Other Essays by Arnold Bennett.*

Acknowledgment for permission to quote from copyrighted material is made to the following copyright holders—for the novels of William Golding: Faber & Faber, Coward-McCann, Harcourt, Brace & World, and Mr. Golding; for H. G. Wells's *The Outline of History* (copyright 1920 by H. G. Wells): Professor G. P. Wells, F.R.S.; for the BBC interview of August 28, 1959: Mr. Golding and Mr. Frank Kermode; for the author's discussion of *The Spire,* and *The Pyramid,* first printed as reviews in the *Times Literary Supplement:* the editor, Mr. Arthur Crook.

William Golding

I am very serious. I believe that man suffers from an appalling ignorance of his own nature. I produce my own view, in the belief
that it may be something like the truth. I am fully engaged to the
human dilemma but see it as far more fundamental than a complex
of taxes and astronomy.

William Golding wrote these words in reply to a literary
magazine's questionnaire, "The Writer in His Age." The questionnaire raised the question of "engagement": should the
writer concern himself with the political and social questions
of his time? Golding's answer is unequivocal: the job of the
writer is to show man his image *sub specie aeternitatis*. It is in
this sense of engagement, not to the concerns of the moment
but to what is basic in the human condition, and in the forms
that this engagement has led Golding to create, that his unique-
ness lies; he is *the* novelist of our time for whom the novel
matters because of what it can mean, and what it can do.

In the note from which I quoted above, Golding described
himself as "a citizen, a novelist and a schoolmaster." The latter
term is no longer literally applicable, but there is still a good
deal of both the citizen and the schoolmaster in the novelist.
The citizen is concerned with "the defects of society"; the
schoolmaster is concerned to correct them by proper instruc-
tion; the novelist finds the appropriate forms in which man's
own nature may be embodied, that he may learn to know it.
One consequence of this will-to-instruct is that Golding is an
unusually disciplined, schematic writer; he thinks his novels
out very slowly, and in careful detail (he wrote *Lord of the
Flies*, he said, "as if tracing over words already on the page"),

[3]

and he is willing, even eager, to discuss what they mean. Another consequence is his desire to have his works read with the same kind of conscious intelligence, and his distrust of irrational and intuitive views of literary creation. He clearly thinks of his novels as the expressions of conscious intentions that existed before the writing began. Indeed he has twice spelled out what those intentions were. This does not, of course, imply that they took the form of abstract moral propositions which were then clothed in plot; but it does suggest that for Golding the entire plan of the work, *and* the meaning of that plan, were worked out first—that he started with meaning rather than with character or situation. Golding's own glosses of the meanings of *Lord of the Flies* and *Pincher Martin* have not seemed satisfactory to most readers—the teller in fact supports Lawrence's view of the creative process, and not Golding's; nevertheless, the fact that Golding thinks of his books as he does tells us something useful about the forms that they have taken.

There is no adequate critical term for that form. Golding himself has called his books both *myths* and *fables*, and both terms do point to a quality in the novels that it is necessary to recognize—that they are unusually tight, conceptualized, analogical expressions of moral ideas. Still, neither term is quite satisfactory, because both imply a degree of abstraction and an element of the legendary that Golding's novels simply do not have, and it seems better to be content with calling them simply *novels*, while recognizing that they have certain formal properties that distinguish them from most current fiction.

The most striking of these properties is that Golding so patterns his narrative actions as to make them the images of ideas, the imaginative forms of generalizations; the form itself, that is to say, carries meaning apart from the meanings implied by character or those stated more or less didactically by the author. "In all my books," Golding has said, "I have suggested a

shape in the universe that may, as it were, account for things."
To direct the attentions of his readers to that shape,
Golding has chosen situations that isolate what is basic, and
avoid both the merely topical and the subjective existence of
the author. All but two of his novels employ a situation that is
remote in time or space, characters who are radically unlike
the author, and a narrative tone that is removed, analytical, and
judicial. Consequently we must look for human relevance to
the patterned action itself; if we "identify," it must be with
the moral—with the conception of man and the shape of the
universe—and not with this character or that one.

The forms that Golding uses carry implications both for the
kind of action selected and for the kind of characters involved
in it. Since Golding proposes to embody general truths in his
novels, he is committed, one would think, to select those human experiences that can be viewed as *exemplary*, not merely
as *typical;* it is not enough to propose that a fictional event
might happen. To be justifiable in a Golding novel an event
must also bear its share of the patterned meaning. Consequently
the novels tend on the whole to be short and densely textured,
and the characters, while they are usually convincingly three-
dimensional human beings, may also function as exemplars of
facets of man's nature—of common sense, or greed, or will (one
of Golding's most impressive gifts is his ability to make characters exemplify abstractions without *becoming* abstractions).

What we acknowledge if we choose to call Golding a
fabulist is not that the total story is reducible to a moral
proposition—this is obviously not true—but rather that he
writes from clear and strong moral assumptions, and that those
assumptions give form and direction to his fictions. But if
Aesop and La Fontaine wrote fables, we need another term
for Golding. We might borrow one from scholastic aesthetics,
and call them *tropological*, meaning by this that the novels

individually "suggest a shape in the universe," and are constructed as models of such moral shapes. Or if tropological seems too rarefied, *moral models* will do. The point, in any case, is to suggest the patterned quality of Golding's work, and to recognize the assumptions which that quality implies. Golding accepts certain traditional ideas about man and his place in the world: that mind, by meditation and speculation, may arrive at truth; that it may find in the past, meanings which are relevant to the present, and available through memory; that it may appropriately concern itself with metaphysics and with morals. Not all of these ideas are current now, certainly not in the avant-garde, and consequently Golding's work may seem, in the context of his time, more didactic and moralizing than in fact it is. For though Golding is a moralist, he is not a moral-maker, and his novels belong, not with Aesop's fables, but with the important symbolic novels of our century—with Camus's and Kafka's.

Golding has founded *Lord of the Flies* on a number of more or less current conventions. First of all, he has used the science-fiction convention of setting his action in the future, thus substituting the eventually probable for the immediately actual, and protecting his fable from literalistic judgments of details or of credibility. A planeload of boys has been evacuated from an England engaged in some future war fought against "the reds"; after their departure an atomic bomb has fallen on England, and civilization is in ruins. The plane flies south and east, stopping at Gibraltar and Addis Ababa; still farther east —over the Indian Ocean, or perhaps the Pacific, the plane is attacked by an enemy aircraft, the "passenger tube" containing the boys is jettisoned, and the rest of the plane crashes in flames. The boys land unharmed on a desert island.

At this point, a second literary convention enters. The

[6]

desert island tale shares certain literary qualities with science fiction. Both offer a "what-would-happen-if" situation, in which real experience is simplified in order that certain values and problems may be regarded in isolation. Both tend to simplify human moral issues by externalizing good and evil; both offer occasions for Utopian fantasies. Golding's most immediate source is R. M. Ballantyne's *Coral Island*, a Victorian boys' book of South Sea adventure, but Ballantyne didn't invent the island dream; that dream began when man first felt the pressures of his civilization enough to think that a life without civilization might be a life without problems.

The relation of Golding's novel to Ballantyne's is nevertheless important enough to pause over. In *Coral Island*, three English boys called Ralph, Jack, and Peterkin are shipwrecked on a tropical island, meet pirates and cannibals, and conquer all adversities with English fortitude and Christian virtue. We may say that *Coral Island* is a clumsy moral tale, in which good is defined as being English and Christian and jolly, and especially an English Christian *boy*, and in which evil is unchristian, savage, and adult. The three boys are rational, self-reliant, inventive, and virtuous—in short, they are like no boys that anyone has ever known.

Golding regards *Coral Island* morality as unrealistic, and therefore not truly moral, and he has used it ironically in his own novel, as a foil for his own version of man's moral nature. In an interview Golding described his use of Ballantyne's book in this way:

What I'm saying to myself is "don't be such a fool, you remember when you were a boy, a small boy, how you lived on that island with Ralph and Jack and Peterkin." . . . I said to myself finally, "Now you are grown up, you are adult; it's taken you a long time to become adult, but now you've got there you can see that people are not like that; they would not behave like that if they were God-fearing English gentlemen, and they went to an island like that."

[7]

There savagery would not be found in natives on an island. As like as not they would find savages who were kindly and uncomplicated and that the devil would rise out of the intellectual complications of the three white men on the island itself.

One might say that *Lord of the Flies* is a refutation of *Coral Island*, and that Golding sets about to show us that the devil rises, not out of pirates and cannibals and such alien creatures, but out of the darkness of man's heart. The *Coral Island* attitude exists in the novel—Jack sounds very like Ballantyne's Jack when he says: "After all, we're not savages. We're English; and the English are best at everything." And the naval commander who rescues the boys at the end of the book speaks in the same vein: "I should have thought that a pack of British boys—you're all British aren't you?—would have been able to put up a better show than that—I mean—" But Jack and the commander are wrong; the pack of British boys are in fact cruel and murderous savages who reduce the island to a burning wreckage and destroy the dream of innocence.

The fable of the novel is a fairly simple one. The boys first set out to create a rational society modeled on what "grown-ups" would do. They establish a government and laws, they provide for food and shelter, and they light a signal fire. But this rational society begins to break down almost at once, under two instinctual pressures—fear and blood lust. The dark unknown that surrounds the children gradually assumes a monstrous identity, and becomes "the beast," to be feared and propitiated; and hunting for food becomes killing. The hunters break away from the society, and create their own primitive, savage, orgiastic tribal society. They kill two of the three rational boys, and are hunting down the third when the adult world intervenes.

This fable, as sketched, is susceptible of several interpretations, and Golding's critics have found it coherent on a number of levels, according to their own preoccupations. Freudians have found in the novel a conscious dramatization of psychological theory: "denied the sustaining and repressing authority of parents, church and state, [the children] form a new culture the development of which reflects that of genuine primitive society, evolving its gods and demons (its myths), its rituals and taboos (its social norms)." The political-minded have been able to read it as "the modern political nightmare," in which rational democracy is destroyed by irrational authoritarianism ("I hope," said V. S. Pritchett, "this book is being read in Germany"). The social-minded have found in it a social allegory, in which life, without civilized restraints, becomes nasty, brutish, and short. And the religious have simply said, in a complacent tone, "Original Sin, of course."

It is, of course, entirely possible that Golding has managed to construct a fable that does express all these ideas of evil, and that what we are dealing with is not alternative interpretations, but simply levels of meaning. The idea of Original Sin, for example, does have political, social, and psychological implications; if it is true that man is inherently prone to evil, then certain conclusions about the structure of his relations to other men would seem to follow. The idea of Original Sin seems, indeed, to be one of the "great commonplaces," one of those ideas which are so central to man's conception of himself that they turn up, in one form or another, in almost any systematic account of human nature. It describes one of perhaps two possible accounts of the nature of human behavior (*Coral Island* assumes the other one).

Since the novel is symbolic, the best approach would seem to be to examine first the "meaning" of each of the major characters, and then to proceed to consider the significance of their interactions. Ralph—in *Coral Island* the first-person narrator—here provides the most consistent point of view, because he most nearly speaks for us, rational, fallible humankind; Ralph is the man who accepts responsibility that he is not particularly

[9]

fitted for because he sees that the alternative to responsibility is savagery and moral chaos. He tries to establish and preserve an orderly, rational society; he takes as his totem the conch, making it the symbol of rational, orderly discussion.

Ralph's antagonist is Jack, who represents "the brilliant world of hunting, tactics, fierce exhilaration, skill," as Ralph represents "the world of longing and baffled common-sense." Between them there is an "indefinable connection"; like Cain and Abel, they are antithetical, but intimately linked together —man-the-destroyer confronting man-the-preserver. Jack is the hunter, the boy who becomes a beast of prey (and who uses *kill* as an intransitive verb, an act which is for him an end in itself). He is also the dictator, the authoritarian man-of-power who enters the scene like a drill sergeant, who despises assemblies and the conch, and who becomes in the end an absolute ruler of his tribe. He devises the painted mask of the hunter, behind which a boy may hide, "liberated from shame and self-consciousness," and by painting the boys he turns them into an anonymous mob of murderous savages, "a demented but partly secure society." Jack is the first of the bigger boys to accept "the beast" as possible, and the one who offers the propitiatory sacrifice to it; he is the High Priest of Beelzebub, the Lord of the Flies.

Associated with each of these antagonists is a follower who represents in a more nearly allegorical form the principal value of his leader. Piggy, Ralph's "true, wise friend," is a scientific-minded rationalist, who models his behavior on what he thinks grownups would do, and scorns the other children for "acting like a crowd of kids." He can think better than Ralph, and in a society in which thought was enough he would be supremely valuable; but on the island he is ineffectual; he is incapable of action, and is a physical coward. His totem is his spectacles, and with them he is the fire-bringer; but when Jack

[10]

first breaks one lens and then steals the other, Piggy becomes blind and helpless, a bag of fat. His trust in the power and wisdom of grownups is itself a sign of his inadequacy; for if the novel makes one point clearly, it is that adults have no special wisdom, and are engaged in a larger scale, but equally destructive, version of the savage game that the hunters play. (When Ralph wishes that the outer world might "send us something grown-up . . . a sign or something," the adult world obliges with the dead parachutist, an image of terror that destroys Ralph's rational society.)

Beside or slightly behind Jack stands Roger, around whom clings "the hangman's horror." Roger's lust is the lust for power over living things, the power to destroy life. In the beginning he is restrained by "the taboo of the old life . . . the protection of parents and school and policemen and the law." Jack and the paint of savagery liberate Roger from these taboos, and "with a sense of delirious abandonment" he rolls the rock down the cliff, killing Piggy, his opposite.

One character, the most difficult to treat, remains. Simon, the shy visionary, perceptive but inarticulate, occupies a central position in the symbolic scheme of the book. It is Simon who first stammers that perhaps the beast is "only us," who sees the beast in terms of "mankind's essential illness," and who goes alone to confront *both* beasts, the grinning pig's head and the rotting airman, because, as he says, "What else is there to do?" Golding has described Simon as a saint, "someone who voluntarily embraces this beast, goes . . . and tries to get rid of him and goes to give the good news to the ordinary bestial man on the beach, and gets killed for it." He would appear to be, then, at least in Golding's intentions, the embodiment of moral understanding. If this is so, those symbolic scenes in which he appears will be crucial to an understanding of the novel.

I have said that one distinction between Golding's novels

and allegory is that the novels are meaning-in-action, general truth given narrative or dramatic form by the creative imagination. In considering the meaning of *Lord of the Flies*, one cannot therefore stop at an examination of character—meaning must emerge from character-in-action. In the narrative action certain scenes stand out as crucial, and most of these announce their importance by being overtly symbolic. There is, for example, a series of scenes in which Jack's hunters evolve a ritual dance. On the first occasion, in Chapter 4, a child *pretends* to be the pig, and the hunters *pretend* to beat him. A chapter later the dance has become crueler, "and littluns that had had enough were staggering away, howling." After the next hunt Robert, acting the pig in the dance, squeals with real pain, and the hunters cry "Kill him! Kill him!" After the dance the boys discuss ways of improving the ritual: " 'You want a real pig,' said Robert, still caressing his rump, 'because you've got to kill him.'

" 'Use a littlun,' said Jack, and everybody laughed." In the final ritual dance, the sacrificial function is acknowledged; the boys' chant is no longer "Kill the pig," but "Kill the *beast!*" and when Simon crawls from the forest, the boys fulfill their ritual sacrifice, and by killing a human being, make themselves beasts ("there were no words, and no movements but the tearing of teeth and claws"). Ironically, they have killed the one person who could have saved them from bestiality, for Simon has seen the figure on the mountaintop, and knows that the beast is "harmless and horrible."

Simon's lonely, voluntary quest for the beast is certainly the symbolic core of the book. The meaning of the book depends on the meaning of the beast, and it is that meaning that Simon sets out to determine. His first act is to withdraw to a place of contemplation, a sunlit space in the midst of the forest. It is to the same place that Jack and his hunters bring the pig's head, and leave it impaled on a stick as a sacrifice to the beast they fear. When they have gone, Simon holds halucinatory conversation with the Lord of the Flies, Beelzebub, the Lord of Filth and Dung. The head, "with the infinite cynicism of adult life," assures Simon that "everything was a bad business," and advises him to run away, back to the other children, and to abandon his quest. "I'm part of you," it tells him (in words that echo Simon's own "maybe it's only us"), "I'm the reason why it's no go." Simon, apparently epileptic, falls in a fit. But when he wakes, he turns upward, toward the top of the mountain, where the truth lies. He finds the airman, rotting and fly-blown, and tenderly frees the figure from the wind's indignity. Then he sets off, weak and staggering, to tell the other boys that the beast is human, and is murdered by them.

How are we to interpret this sequence? We may say, first of all, that the beast symbolizes the source of evil in human life. Either it is something terrifying and external, which cannot be understood but must simply be lived with (this is Jack's version), or it is a part of man's nature, "only us," in which case it may be understood, and perhaps controlled by reason and rule. Simon understands that man must seek out the meaning of evil ("what else is there to do?"). By seeking, he comes to know it, "harmless and horrible." Thus far the moral point seems orthodox enough. But when he tries to tell his understanding to others, they take *him* for the beast, and destroy him in terror. Another common idea, though a more somber one—men fear the bearers of truth, and will destroy them. This has both political and psychological implications. A "demented but partly secure society" (read: Nazi Germany, or any authoritarian nation) will resist and attempt to destroy anyone who offers to substitute reason and responsible individual action for the irresponsible, unreasoning, *secure* action of the mass. And in psychological terms, the members of a "demented society" may create an irrational, external evil, and in its name commit deeds that as rational men they could not tolerate (the history of modern persecutions offers examples enough); such a society *has* to destroy the man who says, "The evil is in yourselves."

At this point, I should like to return to the argument that this novel is a symbolic form but not an allegory. One aspect of this distinction is that Golding has written a book that has a dense and often poetic verbal texture, in which metaphor and image work as they do in poetry, and enrich and modify the bare significances of the moral form. Golding's treatment of Simon's death is a particularly good case in point. At this instant, a storm breaks, the wind fills the parachute on the mountain, and the figure, freed by Simon, floats and falls toward the beach, scattering the boys in terror before passing out to sea. The storm ends, stars appear, the tide rises. Stars above and phosphorescent sea below fill the scene with brightness and quiet.

Along the shoreward edge of the shallows the advancing clearness was full of strange, moonbeam-bodied creatures with fiery eyes. Here and there a larger pebble clung to its own air and was covered with a coat of pearls. The tide swelled in over the rain-pitted sand and smoothed everything with a layer of silver. Now it touched the first of the stains that seeped from the broken body and the creatures made a moving patch of light as they gathered at the edge. The water rose farther and dressed Simon's coarse hair with brightness. The line of his cheek silvered and the turn of his shoulder became sculptured marble. The strange attendant creatures, with their fiery eyes and trailing vapors, busied themselves round his head. The body lifted a fraction of an inch from the sand and a bubble of air escaped from the mouth with a wet plop. Then it turned gently in the water.

Somewhere over the darkened curve of the world the sun and moon were pulling, and the film of water on the earth planet was held, bulging slightly on one side while the solid core turned. The great wave of the tide moved farther along the island and the water lifted. Softly, surrounded by a fringe of inquisitive bright creatures, itself a silver shape beneath the steadfast constellations, Simon's dead body moved out toward the open sea.

[14]

This is Golding's rhetoric at its richest, but it works. The imagery of light and value—*moonbeam, pearls, silver, bright-ness, marble*—effect a transfiguration, by which the dead child is made worthy, his death an elevation. In terms of allegory, this sort of metaphorical weighting would perhaps be imprecise and deceptive; in terms of a symbolic novel, it seems to me a legitimate application of a skillful writer's art.

In discussing the actions of *Lord of the Flies* I have again and again slipped from talking about boys to describing the characters as men, or simply as human beings. It is true that as the action rises to its crises—to the *agon* of Chapter 5, Simon's confrontation with the beast, the murders, the final hunt—we cease to respond to the story as a story about children, and see them simply as *people*, engaged in desperate, destructive actions. Consequently, Golding can achieve a highly dramatic effect at the end of the book by bringing our eyes down, with Ralph's, to a beach-level view of an adult, and then swinging round, to show us Ralph from the adult's point of view. The result is an irony that makes two points. First, we see with sudden clarity that these murderous savages were civilized children; the point is not, I take it, that children are more horrid than we thought (though they are), but rather that the human propensity for evil knows no limits, not even limits of age, and that there is no Age of Innocence (Ralph weeps for the end of innocence, but when did it exist, except as an illusion made of his own ignorance?). Second, there is the adult, large, efficient, confident—the "grown-up" that the children have wished for all along. But his words show at once that he is a large, stupid *Coral Island* mentality in a peaked cap, entirely blind to the moral realities of the situation. He may save Ralph's life, but he will not understand. And once he has gathered up the castaways, he will return to his ship, and the grown-up business of hunting men (just as the boys have been hunting Ralph). "And who," asks Golding, "will rescue the adult and his cruiser?"

To return briefly to the question of levels of interpretation: it seems clear that *Lord of the Flies* should be read as a moral novel embodying a conception of human depravity which is compatible with, but not limited to, the Christian doctrine of Original Sin. To call the novel religious is to suggest that its values are more developed, and more affirmative, than in fact they are; Golding makes no reference to Grace, or to Divinity, but only to the darkness of men's hearts, and to the God of Dung and Filth who rules there. Simon is perhaps a saint, and sainthood is a valuable human condition, but there is no sign in the novel that Simon's sainthood has touched any soul but his own. The novel tells us a good deal about evil; but about salvation it is silent.

The Inheritors is Golding's most brilliant tour de force—a novel written from the point of view of Neanderthal man. Golding has set himself the task of rendering experience as it would be apprehended by this subhuman, subrational intelligence, and his success, within the severe limits implied, is extraordinary. But, being Golding, he has not assumed such difficulties simply to demonstrate his skills; *The Inheritors*, like *Lord of the Flies*, is a moral fable, and the quality of the observing consciousness employed is a part of the morality.

The Inheritors also resembles *Lord of the Flies* in the way it relates to a book out of Golding's childhood. *Lord of the Flies* used Ballantyne's *Coral Island*, not as a source of plot or character, but as the embodiment of an attitude—a symbol out of childhood of a whole set of wrong beliefs about good and evil. *The Inheritors* uses H. G. Wells's *Outline of History* in a similar way. Wells, in the eighth and ninth chapters of his book, described Neanderthal man, and his extermination by

Homo sapiens. The key passage, from which Golding drew the epigraph to his novel, is this:

We know nothing of the appearance of the Neanderthal man, but this absence of inter-mixture [with *Homo sapiens*] seems to suggest an extreme hairiness, an ugliness, or a repulsive strangeness in his appearance over and above his low forehead, his beetle brows, his ape neck, and his inferior stature. Or he—and she—may have been too fierce to tame. Says Sir Harry Johnston, in a survey of the rise of modern man in his *Views and Reviews:* "The dim racial remembrance of such gorilla-like monsters, with cunning brains, shambling gait, hairy bodies, strong teeth, and possibly cannibalistic tendencies, may be the germ of the ogre in folklore. . . ."

One can see how Wells, with his rationalist's faith in evolution and the virtues of "an intelligence very like our own" would be unpalatable to a man like Golding. In an interview Golding described the *Outline* as "the rationalist gospel in excelsis," and went on to recount his reaction when he returned, as an adult, to Wells's book:

When I re-read it as an adult I came across his picture of Neander-thal man, our immediate predecessors, as being these gross brutal creatures who were possibly the basis of the mythological bad man, whatever he may be, the ogre. I thought to myself that this is just absurd. What we're doing is externalising our own inside. We're saying, "Well, he must have been like that, because I don't want to be like it, although I know I am like it."

We might say, then, that Golding and Wells are most basically opposed in their views of the nature of "the ogre"; Wells, the rationalist, wishes to separate this figure of terror from Homo sapiens, and to place him in a repulsive, hairy body, now extinct except in folklore; Golding says the ogre is in our own insides. The two positions are essentially antithetical ideas of the nature of evil: the rationalistic, and the religious. Golding has used a view which he deplores as a foil for his own.

Neanderthal and "true men" are the antagonists of Golding's novel; the plot is summarized in one sentence of Wells:

[17]

Finally, between 40,000 and 25,000 years ago, as the Fourth Glacial Age softened towards more temperate conditions . . . a different human type came upon the scene, and, it would seem, exterminated *Homo Neanderthalensis.*

The Inheritors is an account of that extermination, seen from the point of view of the exterminated. In creating his two primitive species, Golding has on the whole been anthropologically accurate, but he has taken certain significant liberties. He says of his Neanderthals that they have opposed toes, and have not learned to shape the stones that they use for tools; he says of Homo sapiens that he can make clay vessels, bone instruments, and canoes. He has made Neanderthal man *more* primitive, and Homo sapiens more advanced, thus emphasizing the intellectual and cultural gap between the species. And he has widened that gap in order to construct, out of Wells's one-sentence plot, an anthropological version of the Fall of Man.

Virtually the entire novel is narrated from the point of view of Neanderthal men, "the people." We see them first, we observe their tribal behavior, and then only gradually are we made aware of another species. Golding sets out to make two basic points about the people: the quality of their intelligence and (a related point) the quality of their innocence. They are introduced in migration from winter to summer quarters, and immediately a problem arises—a log across a marsh, which they have always used as a bridge, is gone; how are they to cross the water, which they fear? They are baffled, they cannot think consecutively, their minds wander, they have little command of either memory or causality. Finally, Mal, their old leader, remembers a wise man who *made* a bridge with a fallen log, and the people are able to resume their journey, though Mal falls into the water, and later dies of the exposure. The episode of the log is important to the novel as a model of the Neanderthal mind; the most significant feature of that mind is this, that it cannot conceive of relationships, and we might take this as a tentative definition of the State of Innocence: man cannot sin until he can both remember and anticipate.

The innocence of the people is dramatized in a number of ways. We see Lok and his mate, Fa, hunting for food; they find a doe killed by a cat, and take the carcass for food, but only after Fa has said, "A cat has sucked all her blood. There is no blame." Far from being the cannibals that Wells describes, these creatures have a reverence for life that forbids killing or eating blood, and they dislike the taste of meat. Their deity, Oa, is an earth goddess who gives and preserves life, and who is worshiped in natural forms—a root shaped like a woman, and female-looking ice formations. And—one further aspect of their innocence—they share a collective identity that is not yet fully differentiated into separate personalities; thus they share thoughts and emotions, and lack the antagonisms that personalities imply.

Into this prelapsarian collective consciousness there gradually intrudes a sense of "other"—another mysterious species somewhere near. The way in which Golding slowly builds this awareness in the minds of the people gives to his novel some of the excitement of other fictional forms involving unknown antagonists—mystery novels, for instance, and ghost stories use similar devices of dramatic anticipation. Beginning with the missing log (what hands moved it, and why?), Golding offers a series of hints and mysteries, as baffling to us as to the clumsy minds through which we experience them. Lok, for example, smells what he takes to be the fire that the old woman carries on their migration. He turns toward it, and almost falls over a cliff. There is another fire, then, but Lok cannot imagine this, and we are left with his bafflement and fright. Gradually "other" becomes defined—first a scent, than a creature, a lump, a nobody, and finally "the new people."

[19]

The new people are simply *us*—postlapsarian man, with all his capacities for creation and for evil, his fears and desires and guilts. For most of the novel we see these creatures from the outside, with the eyes of innocence. But not really—rather, we receive the data of those innocent eyes, and interpret it as our own familiar behavior. The crucial scene in this respect is the long sequence, taking up almost a quarter of the book, in which Lok and Fa, hidden in a tree, watch an encampment of the new people, and uncomprehendingly witness lust, drunkenness, cruelty, cannibalism—a Goldingesque demonstration of the benefits of "an intelligence very like our own." We also observe the new people's religion, and the contrast to the worship of Oa is significant. The new people's religion is totemic —a man dressed as a stag, a stag drawn on the earth—and sacrificial—the stag requires an amputated finger from a victim chosen by lot. The point seems to be that while innocence can worship natural forms, and the principle of life itself, fallen man constructs mimetic religions, which at least in part worship his *own* capacity to mime, and that his deity is male (in this book the females preserve, the males act and destroy).

The ultimate effect of the meeting of these species is, as Wells said so casually, the extermination of *Homo Neanderthalensis;* but the intermediate effects of their awareness of each other are also significant. The feelings of the people toward the new men are powerful and ambivalent: Lok thinks that "the other people with their many pictures were like water that at once horrifies and at the same time dares and invites a man to go near it. He was obscurely aware of this attraction without definition and it made him foolish." *Pictures* is the Neanderthal's word for thought, and the attraction that the others have is clearly the attraction that knowledge (including the knowledge of good and evil) holds out to innocence. Being innocent, the people do not understand any fear that is

[20]

not a physical response to a physical threat; they surrender to "the indefinable attraction of the new people," but they do so "with a terrified love."

The effect of contact with knowledge is necessarily the loss of innocence; after Lok and Fa have watched the new people's orgy, they creep into the abandoned camp, where they get drunk on mead and discover lust. But experience also teaches Lok to think; out of loss and suffering and responsibility he discovers the basic element of thought—likeness. But the only use to which he can put this new tool is to understand the irresistible power of the new people; "they are like the river and the fall," he thinks, "they are a people of the fall; nothing stands against them." And indeed they are the people of the Fall—that is what the novel is about.

For most of the novel we see the new men's reaction to the people only from a distance; we know that they are frightened, and that they try to destroy what they fear, but only at the end of the novel, when the last of the people lies dead, and the new men are in flight, do we know the nature and extent of their fear. They have discovered objective images of their terrors, and have called them devils, and in their terror they have committed evil deeds that have changed them—a child has gone mad, and a woman is literally possessed of a devil. They are fleeing from the darkness that will henceforth be man's symbol for what he fears, though what he fears is not really back there in the forest—it is, as *Lord of the Flies* tells us, "the darkness of men's hearts." Tuami, the new man, is looking into the still unwritten history of his species when, in the last paragraph of the book, he looks at the line of darkness along the horizon.

It was far away and there was plenty of water in between. He peered forward past the sail to see what lay at the other end of the lake, but it was so long, and there was such a flashing from the water that he could not see if the line of darkness had an ending.

The moral of the novel is not a very complicated one, and certainly it is not what one critic has called it, "blazingly heretical." It offers an anthropological analogue of the Fall, which distinguishes between prelapsarian and postlapsarian man in terms of knowledge of evil and capacity for thought. The book is original in that no one had previously thought of Neanderthal man as a possible analogue for Adam, but the originality is in the fictional conception of the moral, not in the theology (which in a novel is surely as it ought to be). This originality is also the novel's limitation: in so far as *The Inheritors* is an imaginative creation of primitive consciousness it is an unusual achievement, but it is an achievement that succeeds *by* limitation. Golding has written a novel in which his principal perceivers cannot understand or reason about what they perceive, and has thus denied himself the use of important areas of discourse traditionally open to the novelist—introspection and abstract thought cannot be directly expressed as parts of the characters' conscious activities. And since introspection and abstraction are parts of our usual mental equipment, the discourse of *The Inheritors* is strange to us, and sometimes extremely obscure. It is also occasionally rather grotesque in the locutions that it contrives in order to avoid anything that might be construed as reasoning, as when Lok "watched the water run out of her eyes." Is weeping so difficult an abstraction?

But if the style imposes limitations, it also has its expressive strengths. The innocent eye sees actions that we might regard as common for the first time, and the newness becomes a part of our own awareness—as when, for example, Lok and Fa look down from their tree upon human evil. And because Golding is a poetic writer, his treatment of the unfiltered sense data of these innocents is often poetically moving, as when Lok hunts for his lost mate, or when the people bury their old leader, Mal. But beyond these advantages, the point of view of the novel provides another that is perhaps even more essential—the limited perceptions of the observing characters make possible an informing mode of dramatic irony that is steadily and powerfully effective. Dramatic irony depends upon our recognition of limits in characters' perceptions—limits to which we are superior; in *The Inheritors* we observe as Neanderthal man observes, but we interpret as rational, fallen man interprets. Thus we see, from the first action of the novel, that innocence is doomed to yearn toward and be destroyed by thinking, guilty experience. Then in the last chapter Golding cunningly reverses the point of view, and establishes a new irony as Homo sapiens, fleeing his own inner darkness, looks back in terror at the forest of innocence, the remembrance of which "may be the germ of the ogre in folklore . . ." The final irony is in the way the Wellsian epigraph has been realized.

The Inheritors is, as I have said, an extraordinary tour de force, and one which could scarcely be repeated. But one of Golding's virtues as a novelist has been his eagerness to regard each novel as a new approach to new problems, and his unwillingness to imitate himself. "It seems to me," he has said, "that there's really very little point in writing a novel unless you do something that either you suspected you couldn't do, or which you are pretty certain that nobody else has tried before." Both of these conditions are met by *The Inheritors;* both apply equally to Golding's third novel, *Pincher Martin,* a novel with a single character, who dies on page two.

Both formally and intellectually, *Pincher Martin* is the most impressive of Golding's novels. It is also the most difficult, because its form is an involved representation of time and consciousness, and because what it has to say about death is heterodox and complex. It bears certain family resemblances to the two preceding novels: it uses the literature of survival in much the same way that *Lord of the Flies* uses island litera-ture, and it treats an unusual condition of consciousness, as *The Inheritors* does. Like the earlier two, it is a novel with a moral "program," which deals schematically with the problem of evil and its consequences.

But it is also different from the others in important ways. The primary difference is that the form of *Pincher Martin* does not compel a moral interpretation from the beginning; rather it offers first a vivid survival-adventure, and then re-verses itself, and says: What you have been taking as objec-tively true is in fact false—or true in another, paradoxical sense. This is an uncommon fictional technique, but by no means a unique one; satires like *Gulliver's Travels* play tricks with our expectations, and so do the symbolical tales of Poe and Kafka. The difference in Golding's technique is that he goes to considerable trouble to make the apparent seem par-ticularly real *before* he allows the symbolic quality of the ac-tion to appear overtly. As a result the grounds of reality shift within the novel, and the reader's relation to the action is un-stable and ambiguous; this in turn compels a more attentive reading (or rereading) of the book—the symbolic meaning is more difficult to grasp, because it appears in the final chapters as a *new* interpretation of data which we have already inter-preted in a conventional, realistic way.

The action of the novel thus divides into two parts, with a coda. The first part takes Christopher Martin from the mo-ment when a torpedo blows him off the bridge of his destroyer through the events of his efforts to survive on a barren rock. In these ten chapters Golding creates, in sharp, circumstantial detail, the conditions in which Martin's extraordinary will-to-survive operates. The sea, the rock, the creatures that live on it, the weather—all are meticulously set down. So, too, is Pincher Martin, fiercely acting out his ego; and the vividness with which Golding has drawn this figure is in itself a remarkable achievement, since we do not see Pincher's personality reflected from any other human being, but only in relation to hostile nature, and to itself.

This lonely survivor we must regard as admirable, simply because he clings to life so tenaciously, and against such odds (how can we *not* side with Man, against Nature?). His endurance, his will, his ingenuity are all heroic—he is man opposing adversity, refusing to be annihilated. And when he cries "I am Prometheus," we see what he means—he is a man trapped on a barren rock, defying the fate that put him there.

But woven into this heroic narrative are flashbacks of Martin's past that establish a character who is the opposite of heroic—an unscrupulous egoist who has stopped at no depravity, no betrayal of love and friendship, to nourish his own ego. By seeing *this* character developed parallel to the Promethean survivor, we are forced to acknowledge that the same qualities that have kept him alive against such odds are the qualities that make him morally repulsive. And so in the middle of the eleventh chapter we face a moral dilemma: on what grounds can we condemn those qualities by which man survives?

The answer comes in the following three chapters, beginning with the moment when Martin looks down into the sea from his rock, and sees a *red* lobster, and realizes that perhaps his whole effort to survive—rock and all—has been a subjective creation, an act of the will asserting itself against necessity. He has invented it all, ingeniously, but not perfectly; he has forgotten that only boiled lobsters are red, and that guano is insoluble, and he has arranged the rocks on which he survives like the teeth in his own mouth. From this point on, the apparent reality of Pincher's survival begins to dissolve, and with it his own surviving personality, until at the end he is reduced to two hands, red and grasping like lobster claws, and symbolic, as his nickname is symbolic, of his essential nature. And then even these claws are worn away, and Pincher Martin as a personality is annihilated.

But what does it all mean? The coda is there to give us some clues. In the last chapter, as in the final chapter of *The Inheritors,* Golding provides a new perspective, a shift in point of view out and away from the agent of the action, by which we can regard the action more deliberately and objectively. We are on an island in the Hebrides when a naval party lands to pick up the body of a drowned sailor (Pincher Martin). An islander, called Campbell, is moved and disturbed by the experience, and asks the officer in charge of the party, "Would you say there was any—surviving? Or is that all?" The officer, like the one at the end of *Lord of the Flies,* misunderstands the question, and replies: "If you're worried about Martin—whether he suffered or not. . . . Then don't worry about him. You saw the body. He didn't even have time to kick off his seaboots."

If Pincher didn't have time to kick off his seaboots, then the moment in the first chapter when he apparently *did* kick them off was illusory, and if that was illusory, then so was everything that came after, and we must go back and reinterpret what we have read. Survival in *Pincher Martin* is not survival in the ordinary sea-story sense after all; Golding has used the "man-against-the-sea" conventions here just as he used the desert island conventions in *Lord of the Flies,* to provide a system of expectations against which to construct a personal and different version of the shape of things.

Some readers have felt cheated by this last-sentence reversal of their assumptions about the nature of reality in the novel. But in fact Golding has placed a number of clues to Pincher's state earlier in the novel, and the seaboots should come as the clincher; the clues are scattered and concealed, like the clues in a mystery novel, in order that the reader should discover the

[26]

truth late in the book, and with surprise, but they are there. This device of discovery is dramatic, but it is more than that; it is a way of making an important point about the meaning of death. Though Martin dies on page two, this physical death is passed over: there are kinds of dying that are more important than that instant of merely physiological change. (Golding's American publisher made this point clearer by calling the novel *The Two Deaths of Christopher Martin*.) An audience for which Campbell's question about eternity was a vital one would surely have no trouble in understanding the paradoxes of living-into-death and dying-into-life that inform the novel; it is only to rational materialists (for whom Pincher is a type) that a novel about varieties of dying will seem an outrageous violation of reality.

Pincher Martin is so tightly and intricately interwoven as to read like a difficult poem; one must attend to its symbols and images in order to understand its narrative action, and indeed there is little that one could call *plot* in the book. The sequence of events is determined, not by the interaction of character and environment as in conventional novels, but by the necessities of the symbolic form in which Golding has expressed his theme. So many readers found this form difficult that when the novel was dramatized on the B.B.C. Third Programme, Golding provided his own account of the theme:

Christopher Hadley Martin had no belief in anything but the importance of his own life; no love, no God. Because he was created in the image of God he had a freedom of choice which he used to centre the world on himself. He did not believe in purgatory and therefore when he died it was not presented to him in overtly theological terms. The greed for life which had been the mainspring of his nature, forced him to refuse the selfless act of dying. He continued to exist separately in a world composed of his own murderous nature. His drowned body lies rolling in the Atlantic but the ravenous ego invents a rock for him to endure on. It is the memory of an aching tooth. Ostensibly and rationally he is a survivor from a torpedoed destroyer: but deep down he knows the truth. He is not fighting for bodily survival but for his continuing identity in face of what will smash it and sweep it away—the black lightning, the compassion of God. For Christopher, the Christbearer, has become Pincher Martin who is little but greed. Just to be Pincher is purgatory; to be Pincher for eternity is hell.

We must, of course, be cautious about accepting an artist's own version of his work; in Golding's case, the novels tend to expand and live beyond his programs. Nevertheless, this account gives a lead into the novel. We may start with the question of what it is to be Pincher.

It is, first of all, simply to be a man called Martin in the Royal Navy; *Pincher* is a nickname habitually attached to seagoing Martins, just as in the American services all Mullinses are called *Moon*. But Pincher *is* a pincher—his Deadly Sin is Greed, and he eats everything he touches. Pincher is a devourer of life, "born with his mouth and his flies open and both hands out to grab." The grabbing hands, which are imaged in the novel as lobsters, are the last part of Pincher to disappear at the end.

This supreme greed is expressed in the novel in a parable, the Parable of the Chinese Box. One of Pincher's victims describes how the Chinese, when they wish to prepare a rare dish, bury a fish in a tin box. Maggots eat the fish, and then one another, until finally "where there was a fish there is now one huge, successful maggot. Rare dish." Pincher is the huge successful maggot, devouring the other maggots and crying, "I'll live if I have to eat everything else on this bloody box!"

Pincher's greed, however, is not a motive in itself; it is the means by which he preserves the only value in his world—his own personality. Those human attributes that assert identity—speech, thought, the consciousness of consciousness—are his goods; and loss of identity—as in sleep and ultimately death—

is his evil. In his past life he has used other people to reassure himself of his own existence, as he has used photographs and mirrors. But on the rock there are no mirrors, and his identity-card photograph is blurred, and there is no one to touch; his existence there is therefore one fierce effort to preserve his personality, to assert that "I am what I always was," and later simply "I am! I am!" Pincher, in his efforts to assert that because he thinks, he is, is simply the modern heir of Descartes, man proving his own existence from the inside out. Starting with mind, he creates his own world in which all meaning and value is in *self;* and all outside self is meaningless mechanism, the material upon which mind plays, and on which self feeds.

This egocentric version of reality not only relates Pincher to the Cartesian tradition; it also connects with his "I am Prometheus." Prometheus is *the* mythic hero of humanistic, liberal man: he is the man-befriender, the God-defier, the indestructible life-worshiping identity whose own existence gives meaning to his suffering, and whose suffering affirms his existence. One might expect that Golding, the disillusioned ex-liberal, would consider Prometheus a symbol of that conception of man which he finds most immoral; and *Pincher Martin* might well be subtitled "The Case Against Prometheus." Golding establishes this point by making Pincher's Promethean heroism simply one more case of his self-creating egoism; Pincher *plays* Prometheus (he is, after all, a professional actor), to appropriate imaginary background music by Tchaikovsky, Wagner, and Holst: "it was not really necessary to crawl," Golding observes, "but the background music underlined the heroism of a slow, undefeated advance against odds." This is not heroism, but a parody of it; and indeed *parody* describes pretty well the overall relationship between what Pincher imagines himself doing and the reality—he is a parody Robinson Crusoe, a parody Hamlet, a parody Lear, a parody

Lucifer. But he is one reality—Pincher, the clutching claws.

Strictly speaking, there is no character in the novel except Pincher; his isolation is complete from beginning to end. The naval officer and Campbell in the last chapter have no particular definition, and even the persons who people Pincher's memories and visions are not really characters, because Pincher has regarded them not as separate human beings but as things to be devoured. One figure, however, stands in an important symbolic relation to Pincher; the existence of his friend Nathaniel is interwoven with Pincher's in the way that good is interwoven with evil, dark with light. Nathaniel is a religious man and something of a mystic; he lectures on "the technique of dying into heaven," and he warns Pincher to prepare for death. Like his Biblical namesake he is a man "in whom is no guile"; no doubt we are also meant to recall Christ's words to Nathaniel: "Hereafter ye shall see heaven open, and the angels of God ascending and descending upon the Son of man." Nathaniel is the opposite of Pincher; he can love selflessly and without thought, and he therefore wins the love of Mary, the girl for whom Pincher feels an obsessive lust.

The most important single scene in the novel is probably the one in which Nathaniel explains his eschatology to an amused Pincher. Man must learn, says Nathaniel, the technique of dying into heaven, in order to make himself ready for heaven when death comes. "Take us as we are now and heaven would be sheer negation," he says. "Without form and void. You see? A sort of black lightning, destroying everything that we call life . . ." If we do not prepare ourselves for heaven (*heaven* here meaning simply eternity described spatially), then we will die into the sort of afterlife that our natures invent. This, it is clear, is what has happened to Pincher; the rock is the heaven he has invented for himself, a barren rock like a tooth, without life except of the lowest sort, a place in which the only possible value is bare survival. Pincher's heaven is the appropriate fate of a man who has lived as he has lived; but because it is his own invention, it is not eternal. It exists by an act of will, and when his will fails, and he admits that he cannot believe in the objective existence of his invention, then the black lightning comes and annihilates him.

The final incident of Pincher's existence is a visionary interview with a mysterious figure in seaman's clothes, who is God. "What do you believe in?" God asks. "The thread of my life," Pincher replies. "I have created you and I can create my own heaven." "You *have* created it," says God. And in God's presence the world of rock and sea stops moving, becomes painted paper, cracks, and drops into "absolute nothingness."

Pincher Martin is an eschatological novel, a myth of dying; nevertheless, it is more concerned with life than with death (perhaps this is true of all such works), and Golding uses the ambiguities of time and reality in Pincher's survival narrative to make moral points about man's attitudes toward death as they affect his attitudes toward life. From the right view of the selfless act of dying, the right moral principles will follow; Nathaniel is a somewhat obscure embodiment of those principles, Pincher of their negation. The central point of the novel seems to be simply this: death is the end of identity. If we accept this, we will prepare for the end of identity, and will value what is personal and individual in our existences less (as saints have always done), and we will fear death less because the loss of identity will be familiar and acceptable to us. Whether indeed we will live in a "heaven" of our own invention if we die unprepared is of no importance, except as a symbolic way of representing the terrors of death to an identity-preserver, a Pincher.

When Golding was asked about the "mythical aspect" of Pincher, he replied that Pincher was "a fallen man . . . Very much fallen—he's fallen more than most. In fact, I went out of my way to damn Pincher as much as I could by making him the most unpleasant, the nastiest type I could think of, and I was very interested to see how critics all over the place said, 'Well, yes, we are like that.' I was really rather pleased." He should not have been surprised that responsive readers found in this "nastiest type" an image of their own natures. Like all of Golding's major characters, Pincher is an embodiment of a proposition about human nature, rather than an individual; in so far as we recognize greed as a sin to which we are prone, we *must* say, "Yes, we are like that."

But this generalized quality in the central figure is also the principal limitation of the novel. Pincher is not a credible, individualized character as we understand character in most fiction; he exists in conditions that strip him of personality—indeed that is the symbolic point of the action—and leave him simply *a* human creature. The rock is the most real thing in the book, and Pincher is most real in his survivor-relation to it; when we see him in flashbacks with other persons he becomes a stock melodramatic villain, the Handsome Seducer. The symbolic action engages us—and engages us with more force than either *Lord of the Flies* or *The Inheritors* does— because it is barer, more entirely symbolic. But it does so at the expense of other expectations that are part of our general feeling for fiction—that there shall be persons with whom we can ally ourselves, existing in a believable world, that we shall experience life being lived. *Pincher Martin* is an extraordinary achievement, a moral document that is also a work of art, in which moral meaning is entirely embodied in artistic form. But its excellence is also its limitation, and it is not an excellence that could be repeated. Clearly Golding had to seek another fictional form for his moral preoccupations; and that is what he did in *Free Fall*.

[32]

Free Fall, Golding's fourth novel, might be regarded as his answer to Kingsley Amis. Amis had said of *Pincher Martin:*

it is the narrowness and remoteness of that world . . . which rob the novel of the universality it appears to claim. Although Martin is in some sense doing duty for man, the context of this performance is too remote from the world of man to excite that continuous recognition and self-recognition upon which depends the novelist's power to persuade.

Perhaps Golding felt this same limitation in his previous work; at any rate, in *Free Fall* he addressed himself, for the first time, to the world of men, and wrote a novel that is immediately striking, to a reader who comes to it from the earlier work, for the density and detail of its social texture. The world of *Free Fall* is ordinary and actual and grimy—and the man through whose eyes we are enabled to see this world is an ordinary, unheroic man who insists on his representativeness. The other novels depended for their expressive power upon a spine of significant action that Golding calls *fable* or *myth;* in *Free Fall* he abandoned that useful device, and wrote a novel in which meaning is embodied in events treated literally, and interpreted in recollection by a first-person narrator. The result is a novel that is slow-paced and reflective, and comparatively speaking, *realistic*—a novel that resembles the novels of Joyce Cary more than it does Golding's earlier work.

The change to a new formal problem is of course characteristic of Golding; certainly no two Golding novels are alike in their specifics, and *Free Fall* is particularly striking in its formal departures. But on the other hand, all the novels are clearly the products of the same "incompetently religious man" (Golding's phrase for himself), and show the same moral preoccupations and themes. *Free Fall* has a notably different surface, but it is concerned, like the other novels, with freedom and necessity, guilt and responsibility, reason and irrationality, and the nature of evil. The principal character, Sammy Mountjoy, is a more attractive man than Christopher Martin, but he has also been a pincher, and his narrative is, like Martin's, a mixture of recollected events and current reflections; only the proportions have been reversed. Pincher Martin's *present* condition is what holds us in that novel, while Sammy Mountjoy's attention is altogether on the past, and his present is sketchy and ambiguous. This reversal is an appropriate one, since Sammy is consciously searching in his past for its meaning; but the point to be made now is that the meanings he finds are consistent and continuous with the previous novels—there is no innovation in ideas.

Free Fall is a long reflection by the narrator upon the events of his past. The events are offered, not as they occurred, but in the order of their importance to Sammy Mountjoy. This ordering is difficult, and sometimes obscure, but if we piece together the details we will arrive at a history for Sammy that will run something like this: born in 1917, in a slum somewhere in Kent, the bastard son of a promiscuous charwoman, father unknown. Adopted, after his mother's death, by the local vicar, and educated in the local grammar school. Went to London to study art, became a painter, and briefly, a member of the Communist Party. During World War II served as a combat artist, was captured by the Nazis and imprisoned. Married, one child. To this should be added two less creditable incidents: as a child, Sammy attempted to desecrate the altar of the parish church; and as a young man he seduced his childhood sweetheart and later abandoned her, perhaps contributing to her eventual madness.

This narrative has chronological sequence, but it has no other pattern, and therefore no meaning. In reexamining his past, Sammy is searching for a pattern which will give experience moral coherence; "I am looking," he says, "for the beginning of responsibility, the beginning of darkness, the point where I began." Man is, in Golding's view, a pattern-making animal; Christianity is a pattern, Marxism is a pattern, scientific rationalism is a pattern. But experience itself is patternless, and it is this fact that provides the central issue of the novel—pattern-making man confronting patternlessness. "The difference between being alive and being an inorganic substance," Golding remarked in an interview in 1958, "is just this proliferation of experience, this absence of pattern." And he went on to say of *Free Fall*, then about to be published, "This time I want to show the patternlessness of life before we impose our patterns on it."

Sammy's particular search is for the answer to one question: "Where did I lose my freedom?" Examining his present moment, he concludes that he is not free—he is the victim of the mechanics of cause and effect. Turning back to his earliest memory, he recalls a moment when he sat in a park at the center of a fan of radiating paths, and knew that he could take any one. At that moment freedom was as real as the taste of potatoes; somewhere between that time and Sammy's present he must have lost his freedom, must have made a choice that ended the possibility of choice. The novel records his search through memory for that decisive moment.

It did not happen in childhood. Sammy examines his early past, and concludes that there is a radical discontinuity between himself and the "infant Samuel" who stole fag-cards from smaller boys and tried to desecrate the altar. It had already begun when he betrayed the love of the innocent Beatrice. As Sammy recalls each episode, he asks himself, "Here?" And replies, "Not here."

There is only one point at which that question does not invoke an immediate and negative answer. At the end of the

[35]

twelfth chapter Sammy, leaving school for the last time, walks in the woods and catechizes himself.

What is important to you? (he asks himself).
"Beatrice Ifor."
She thinks you depraved already. She dislikes you.
"If I want something enough I can always get it provided I am willing to make the appropriate sacrifice."
What will you sacrifice?
"Everything."
Here?

The appropriate sacrifice, it would seem, is freedom; by choosing to involve himself completely in another person ("I want to be you," Sammy tells Beatrice), he has entered the adult world of guilt, and Golding seems to propose that the beginning of guilt is the end of freedom. But such a proposition is scarcely an answer, since it contains a fundamental paradox—without freedom, how can a man be guilty?

The terms of the paradox are apparent in the title of the novel—*Free fall* is both a theological and a scientific reference: it alludes to Adam's (and man's) freedom of choice, and therefore implies a moral thesis; and it also refers to that state of neutralized gravitational pull that is a condition—and a hazard —of space travel, and hence a part of our contemporary scientific mythology. Golding's imagination seems to have been engaged by this idea of man falling freely and endlessly through space, as a metaphor for the scientific conception of man's place in the universe. These two versions of man—the religious and the scientific—oppose each other in the novel, and in Sammy Mountjoy's mind. In his childhood they are represented by two teachers, Nick Shales, the science teacher who is innocent and good and full of love, and Miss Rowena Pringle, the teacher of Religious Knowledge, a sadistic, life-denying spinster. These two, Sammy says, are his "parents not in the flesh," and in so far as Sammy is all of us, the point is obvious enough—we are all the children of science and religion, parents who don't get on together. Sammy sees the two as offering alternative "patterns," either of which would provide a kind of answer to his question, but both of which cannot be true. The objective world that we see and the subjective world that we feel contradict each other—that, I take it, is the point and the problem: "we live in freedom by necessity." The answer that Sammy seeks is really an answer to this paradox.

I have said that the action of *Free Fall* is not fabulous. There is, however, one long central episode that does resemble in form and in forcefulness the actions of the earlier novels. Sammy, a prisoner of war in a German prison camp, is interviewed by Dr. Halde, a Nazi psychologist. Halde is the Devil to Sammy's Christ ("I have taken you up to a pinnacle of the temple," he says, "and shown you the whole earth"); he explains Sammy to himself, and offers him a Nazi answer to his question—a world made tolerable by simplification, a world from which freedom, and therefore guilt, have been eliminated. When Sammy refuses to betray his comrades, Halde has him put in a dark, solitary cell.

The chapter that describes Sammy's terrors in the prison cell is the most powerful in the novel; in its realization of subjective torment it resembles the previous solitary action, that of *Pincher Martin*. Like Martin, Sammy tries to preserve himself by reasoning about his circumstances; and like Martin, he fails. But here the resemblance ends. Pincher ends insanely defying God; Sammy, in his extremity, cries, "Help me! Help me!"

The paragraphs that follow are the most difficult in the novel; they are also the most important. "My life has remained centered," Sammy says, "round the fact of the next few minutes I spent alone and panic-stricken in the dark."

My cry for help was the cry of the rat when the terrier shakes it, a hopeless sound, the raw signature of one savage act. My cry meant no more, was instinctive, said here is flesh of which the nature is to suffer and do thus. I cried out not with hope of an ear but as accepting a shut door, darkness and a shut sky.

But the very act of crying out changed the thing that cried.

Because man cries out instinctively, he can seek for a source of help. In Sammy's circumstances, the physical world offers "neither help nor hope of weakness that might be attacked and overcome"; he cannot escape from the dark cell. He turns to time past, and finds there "only balm for a quieter moment"; the search for the answer through memory has therefore failed, because the past cannot sustain man in the urgency of present need. What is left? Only the future. Sammy "turned therefore and lunged, uncoiled, struck at the future" (in a passage that sounds very like the existential leap into the abyss). When he does so, the cell door bursts open, and he emerges "a man resurrected," who sees the world of matter as infused with miracle—"a universe like a burst casket of jewels." The two worlds of science and belief are still both separate and real, and there is no bridge between them; they are two fields of equal gravitational pull, between which man hangs, in a condition of free fall. "Cause and effect," Sammy thinks.

The law of succession. Statistical probability. The moral order. Sin and remorse. They are all true. Both worlds exist side by side. They meet in me. We have to satisfy the examiners in both worlds at once.

This can scarcely be regarded as a resolution; it is nevertheless an answer, and the only answer that the novel offers. Men live at an intersection of incompatible worlds, both of which they must inhabit; they are both compelled and guilty; they torture each other, but they may also forgive each other. We are all free and falling.

Yeats once wrote that "we assent to the conclusions of reflection but believe what myth presents." This remark provides an apt distinction between *Free Fall* and the preceding novels; the first three are mythlike, and we believe what they present because meaning is embodied in significant action, but *Free Fall* takes as its form "the conclusions of reflection," and we give to those conclusions, at most, our assent. Because Golding has not composed a myth, the action does not carry the meaning, except in the single prison scene, which is different enough in method to seem a violation of the formal unity of the book. Consequently Golding has had to insert passages of generalization and interpretation into Sammy's first-person stream of consciousness. These passages have two unfortunate effects: they expose Golding's ideas to the kind of cold, philosophical scrutiny that one gives to didactic moral writing; and they impede the movement of the novel.

Another apparent flaw in the novel is the order of the incidents. Scene follows scene in a sequence devised for didactic reasons (Sammy tells us that he is recalling past events in order of their importance to his question); but because the scenes do not compose a myth or fable, they must be read, and must find their connections, on the literal level of action. Consequently there are frequently inexplicable gaps in the narrative, and obliquities of narration that seem merely willful. Characters enter obscurely, to be explained only later, actions are darkly alluded to before they occur, and often in a style that seems gratuitously lush and ambiguous.

One must judge cautiously and generously when dealing with a book like *Free Fall*, though; it is recent, it is difficult, and it is the work of a serious writer of demonstrated imaginative gifts. With such a work, critical understanding sometimes grows slowly, and must pass through many minds before it comes to anything like a just judgment. But until that process has taken place, one must record the difficulties, and say tentatively that in this novel Golding's worthy desire not to repeat himself led him astray, and into a form inappropriate to his preoccupations.

The Spire is in many ways a return to the method of the earlier novels. Golding has once more selected a situation that distances and isolates the action; *The Spire* is set in fourteenth-century England, but more than that it is set almost entirely within a cathedral close, which circumscribes the action and restricts the *dramatis personae* as severely as desert island or primitive forest did. It is an action set in the historical past, but the novel is not an historical novel in the ordinary sense of that term: Golding has not attempted to re-create the age of Edward III, or to fill his pages with the kind of contemporary detail that most historical novelists depend on for verisimilitude. He has rather written another symbolic novel, and has used time and cathedral close to preserve a narrative bareness, and to focus attention on the central symbolic action. (He calls attention to the *un*historical character of his novel by calling his cathedral town Barchester, though it is clearly Salisbury.)

The spire of the title is the spire of Salisbury Cathedral, and the principal action of the novel is the building of that spire. Salisbury, as all the guidebooks tell us, is built on marshland without sufficient foundation to support a structure of such weight; the spire nevertheless stands, as it has stood for 600 years, and so it is said to be "built on faith." Such a spire is a symbol of compelling potentialities: it reaches toward heaven, but rises from untrustworthy foundations on earth; it is made by man, in praise of God; it is beautiful and dangerous, and more dangerous as it rises higher; it is a landmark and a lightning rod, it threatens and summons. Golding, starting with the symbol of the spire, has constructed a novel that takes its

[40]

form from the gradual evolution of the symbol's meanings.

The story line of the novel is simple enough: Jocelin, Dean of Barchester Cathedral, believes himself chosen of God to build a spire on the cathedral, and by force of will compels the spire to be built, against the judgment of both clergy and builders. The novel begins with the first stages of construction, and ends with the spire built, and Jocelin dead. But the focus of this story is not either on character or on action, but on symbolic significances; once more, as in the earlier novels, Golding has conceived his own kind of myth. Jocelin dominates the novel, not as a character but as a growing moral awareness; and the spire dominates Jocelin. As he reaches toward the meaning of the spire, so the reader approaches understanding of the meaning of the novel.

Some of the symbolic meanings of the spire are immediately and conventionally apparent. One thinks of Gothic architecture as expressing spiritual aspiration, and this is Jocelin's first understanding of his vision. But the cathedral is also a diagram of man. In its first appearance—a description of a model of the building that occurs in the first chapter—it diagrams physical man, sexual and suffering:

The model was like a man lying on his back. The nave was his legs placed together, the transepts on either side were his arms outspread. The choir was his body; and the Lady Chapel, where now the services would be held, was his head. And now also, springing, projecting, bursting, erupting from the heart of the building, there was its crown and majesty, the new spire.

These meanings—man-as-phallic and man-as-crucified—are not at first clear to Jocelin, but before the spire is built he knows a good deal more about both, and acknowledges that both have played a part in motivating his vision.

But if the cathedral symbolizes man's physical nature, it also symbolizes his spiritual dimension; it is "an image of living, praying man." Jocelin, in moments of self-condemnation, thinks of himself as "a building with a vast cellarage where the rats live" (one recalls the dark symbolic cellar in *Pincher Martin*) but he is also a building with a spire. If he is a suffering animal, he is an animal who can pray.

A final meaning derives from the fact that the spire goes up contrary to all reasonable principles of construction; it is called Jocelin's Folly, but Jocelin tells the master mason:

The folly isn't mine. It's God's Folly. Even in the old days he never asked men to do what was reasonable. Men can do that for themselves. They can buy and sell, heal and govern. But then out of some deep place comes the command to do what makes no sense at all—to build a ship on dry land; to sit among the dung-hills; to marry a whore; to set their son on the altar of sacrifice. Then, if men have faith, a new thing comes.

God commands man to folly, for His sake, and Jocelin understands his compulsion to build the spire as such a command; but God also asks man to sacrifice what he loves most, as He asked Abraham, and this lesson comes late and painfully to Jocelin. The diagram of prayer is also "a diagram of the folly they don't know about"—the folly of sacrifice. Nor can man be sure that the folly he does is indeed done at God's will; Jocelin to the end is uncertain whether he has been moved by true vision, or by vanity, or by the witchcraft of a woman's beauty.

The narrative line on which the emergent meanings of the symbol are developed is the process of building the spire. As the structure rises, a man is killed, and a woman dies in terrible childbirth, and both deaths stem from Jocelin's "dedicated will." Roger, the master mason, becomes a drunken wreck and attempts suicide. Old friendships end, the harmony of the cathedral chapter is broken. Even the social habits of the town and countryside around are altered; new roads lead to the new landmark, and new roads bring new people. Looking out from the tower, Jocelin sees these changes, and muses:

[42]

I thought it would be simple. I thought the spire would complete a stone bible, be the apocalypse in stone. I never guessed in my folly that there would be a new lesson at every level, and a new power.

The principal lesson is that for man there are no simple acts, that in his folly he cannot foresee the consequences of his actions. Because the spire is the work of man, it is built on blood and sin—"there is no innocent work," Jocelin thinks as he lies dying; nevertheless the spire stands, a gesture of assent, in spite of its dark foundations.

The Spire is a novel about vision; vision motivates Jocelin in his obsessive drive toward his goal, the goal itself a symbol in stone of man's capacity to make his visions actual. If the spire is a gesture of assent, it is assent to that proposition. But that assent is not reached easily. The novel is, as I have said, a novel of emergent meanings, not one of inspirational assertions. The meaning of vision develops in the novel, from Jocelin's first joyous confidence in God's imperative to his final complex comprehension.

Vision is simple while it is spiritual; when man tries to transform it into matter, with human hands, vision becomes complex. The principal complexity, as Jocelin learns, is the human cost; the dynamic tension in the novel is drawn in just these terms: *vision* against *cost*, what man wills against what he can endure. The cost for Jocelin is the willful sacrifice of persons he loves to the vision that he wills.

Golding has dealt before with the immorality of *using* human beings: both Pincher Martin and Sammy Mountjoy are guilty of this sin. Jocelin, in his obsession, uses two men and their women, and destroys them; surely this is evil. Yet out of this crime against humanity rises the spire, an act of faith. The point is not simple, but perhaps a consideration of Jocelin's last two thoughts will make it clearer (Golding has emphasized these sentences by setting them in italics): *"There is no innocent work. God knows where God may be"* and *"It's like the appletree."* The latter sentence requires a gloss. Jocelin had earlier described the complication of his vision in terms of a growing plant—"a single green shoot at first, then clinging tendrils, then branches . . ." Later he goes out into the spring sunshine, and sees an appletree:

There was a cloud of angels flashing in the sunlight, they were pink and gold and white; and they were uttering this sweet scent for joy of the light and the air. They brought with them a scatter of clear leaves, and among the leaves a long, black springing thing. His head swam with the angels, and suddenly he understood there was more to the appletree than one branch. It was there beyond the wall, bursting up with cloud and scatter, laying hold of the earth and the air, a fountain, a marvel, an appletree . . .

It's like the appletree: that is, the spire that Jocelin has built has more to it than one miraculous thrust; it touches earth and air, men and angels, corruption and faith. And perhaps the gesture of assent that it makes is simply an assent to this proposition about the mixed nature of man's works, even in praise of God.

If this *is* the moral of *The Spire*, it is neither heterodox nor startling; it emerges naturally and inevitably from the nature of the mythic material, and in this respect makes a more organic novel than was *Free Fall*, with its didactic moral pointing. But this organicism, based as it is on one entirely dominant symbol, has its limiting features too. *The Spire* seems a particularly extreme case of Golding's characteristic mythmaking method—it is, of all the novels, the one that most clearly began with a symbol to be explored. What can the building of a cathedral spire *mean*? The novel is a complex answer to that question. Consequently the spire remains throughout the novel the most vivid presence, as it is in Jocelin's mind.

All of the distinctive formal properties of the novel derive from this fact. There is, first of all, a diminished sense of the actuality of the novel's physical world; the construction of the spire is often treated in meticulous detail, but the men who build it are dim shadows, performing dim actions in undefined space. Characters are drawn largely through their relation to the spire, rather than to each other. There are few strong scenes, and those that are potentially powerful—the tormenting and murder of the verger in the fourth chapter, for example, and the death of his wife in the seventh—are treated sketchily, as if seen by a man with a mind closed by obsession. And indeed that is the mind that sees them; but Golding, by choosing to imitate obsessive preoccupation, has weakened everything in his novel that is not tower or builder—the symbol and the man who learns it.

Each of these judgments would be an indication of serious weakness if applied to a conventional novel, and a novel with all of these limitations would, one might conclude, be a certain failure. But few critical principles are prescriptive; a novel without strong characterization and without effective scenes of interacting personalities lacks two valuable fictional elements, but it may have other compensations. *The Spire* has a magnificent symbol, which grows and accretes meaning and composes in its relationship with its builder a sufficient human meaning. One might say that there is one further symbolic meaning to be added to the meanings already ascribed to the cathedral spire: it is a symbol of the novel that contains it, because though it lacks sufficient fictional foundations, yet it stands.

Golding has testified to his belief that there is no point in repeating old inventions, and each of his novels has been a new kind of verbal contraption. The first five, however, share a common allegorical (or fabulous or mythical) form; the

[45]

sixth disturbs this pleasing uniformity. To the reader familiar with Golding's other novels, *The Pyramid* will astonish by what it is not. It is not a fable, it does not contain evident allegory, it is not set in a simplified or remote world. It belongs to another, more commonplace tradition of English fiction; it is a low-keyed, realistic novel of growing up in a small town—the sort of book H. G Wells might have written if he had been more attentive to his style.

The book is made of three separate episodes in the life of Oliver, son of a dispenser in a provincial town; the dates are from the 1920s to the late 1940s, the locale is Wiltshire (though Golding adopts Trollopian place names, as he did in *The Spire*). The first episode is a traditional one in the fiction of adolescence: young Oliver discovers sex with the daughter of the Town Crier. In the second he reluctantly participates in a farcical amateur performance of the town operatic society. The third—also traditional—is the mature man's return to the town, and his recollections of the spinster who had taught him music.

Among these three episodes there are certain connections of character and scene, but these do not make for a very tightly or very elaborately structured book. The principal unifying element is the theme suggested by the epigraph: "If thou be among people make for thyself love, the beginning and end of the heart." In each episode Oliver is involved with a person who needs, and reaches out for love: Evie, the Town Crier's promiscuous daughter, Mr. De Tracy, the effeminate director of the musical show, and Miss Dawlish, the music teacher. But in each case he fails; he uses Evie, he laughs at De Tracy, and he admits, over Miss Dawlish's grave, that he is glad she is dead. Among people, he has made nothing.

This is a familiar theme in Golding's work: it is the principal argument of the last three novels, and particularly of

[46]

Pincher Martin and *Free Fall*. The method seems at first glance a new departure. However, if one looks back at Golding's earlier work, one can see that his imagination has always had this other, less flashy side. Piggy, in *Lord of the Flies*, is kin to Mr. Polly, and there are realistic episodes and commonplace characters in the other books (excepting, of course, *The Inheritors*). In those novels, Golding had subordinated his realistic imagination to his allegorizing ends, but actuality would thrust itself pushily forward; and it may be, if one reexamines those books in the light of the newest one, that they will appear less diagrammatic than one thought, and that Golding's critics will have to revise their critial vocabularies.

In his essay "On the Crest of the Wave" Golding has written feelingly of the need "for the novel which tries to look at life anew, in a word, for intransigence." *The Pyramid* is one more example of Golding's own intransigence—his refusal to make concessions to our expectations. Each of his novels has been a radical attempt to "look at life anew," and each has altered our sense of the meaning of his work as a whole. As long as Golding goes on writing this intransigence will go on, and final critical judgments of his achievement must wait. And even an assessment of the last term in the series must be understood as conditional upon the next novel, and the next.

SELECTED BIBLIOGRAPHY

PRINCIPAL WORKS OF WILLIAM GOLDING

Poems. London, Macmillan, 1934; New York, Macmillan, 1935.
Lord of the Flies. London, Faber & Faber, 1954; New York, Coward-McCann, 1955.
The Inheritors. London, Faber & Faber, 1955; New York, Harcourt, Brace & World, 1962.
Pincher Martin. London, Faber & Faber, 1956; Harcourt, Brace, 1957 (titled The Two Deaths of Christopher Martin).
The Brass Butterfly. London, Faber & Faber, 1958.
The Spire. London, Faber & Faber, 1964; Harcourt, Brace & World, 1964.
The Hot Gates. London, Faber & Faber, 1965; New York, Harcourt, Brace & World, 1966.
The Pyramid. London, Faber & Faber, 1967; New York, Harcourt, Brace & World, 1967.

CRITICAL WORKS AND COMMENTARY

Baker, James R. William Golding: A Critical Study. New York, St. Martin's, 1965.
Davis, D. M., "Conversation with Golding," *New Republic,* 148 (May 4, 1963), 28–30.
Dick, B. F. William Golding. New York, Twayne, 1967.
Green, Peter, "The World of William Golding," *Review of English Literature,* 1 (April, 1960), 62–72.
Kermode, Frank, "William Golding," in Puzzles and Epiphanies. London, Routledge, 1962, pp. 198–213.
Kinkead-Weekes, Mark, and Ian Gregor. William Golding: A Critical Study. London, Faber & Faber, 1967; New York, Harcourt, Brace & World, 1968.
Nelson, William, ed. William Golding's Lord of the Flies: A Source Book. New York, Odyssey Press, 1963.
Oldsey, B. S., and Stanley Weintraub. The Art of William Golding. New York, Harcourt, Brace & World, 1965.
Peter, John, "Fables of William Golding," *Kenyon Review,* 19 (Fall, 1957), 577–92.

SASHIMI

by Richard Sebra

abdobooks.com

Published by Pop!, a division of ABDO, PO Box 398166,
Minneapolis, Minnesota 55439. Copyright © 2021 by POP, LLC.
International copyrights reserved in all countries. No part
of this book may be reproduced in any form without written
permission from the publisher. Pop!™ is a trademark and logo
of POP, LLC.

Printed in the United States of America, North Mankato,
Minnesota.

082020
012021

Cover Photo: Shutterstock Images
Interior Photos: Shutterstock Images, 1, 5, 6, 10, 14, 17, 18, 19, 22,
23, 26, 29; iStockphoto, 7, 9, 11, 12, 13, 15, 20, 21, 25, 27, 28
Editor: Sophie Geister-Jones
Series Designers: Candice Keimig, Victoria Bates, and Laura
Graphenteen

Library of Congress Control Number: 2019955029
Publisher's Cataloging-in-Publication Data

Names: Sebra, Richard, author.
Title: Sashimi / by Richard Sebra
Description: Minneapolis, Minnesota : POP!, 2021 | Series:
    Cultural cuisine | Includes online resources and index.
Identifiers: ISBN 9781532167799 (lib. bdg.) | ISBN 9781532168895
    (ebook)
Subjects: LCSH: Japanese cooking--Juvenile literature. |
    Raw foods--Juvenile literature. | Ethnic food--Juvenile
    literature. | International cooking--Juvenile literature. |
    Food--Social aspects--Juvenile literature.
Classification: DDC 641.5952--dc23

WELCOME TO
DiscoverRoo!

Pop open this book and you'll find QR codes loaded
with information, so you can learn even more!

Scan this code* and others like
it while you read, or visit the
website below to make this
book pop!

popbooksonline.com/sashimi

*Scanning QR codes requires a web-enabled smart device with a QR code reader app and a camera.

TABLE OF CONTENTS

CHAPTER 1

CUTTING EDGE

It is evening in Tokyo. The streets are crowded as people head home. A family steps into a small restaurant. Inside, a chef holds a sharp knife. In one motion, he slices off a piece of raw fish.

WATCH A VIDEO HERE!

A chef slices salmon for sashimi.

A plate of sashimi often includes several different types of fish.

The chef cuts the fish into many small pieces. He places the pieces on a plate.

He arranges them in a pattern. Then he passes the plate to the hungry family.

Sashimi is a popular dish in Japan. It is similar to **sushi**. But sushi always contains rice. Sashimi is just raw fish.

In sushi, fish can be placed atop rice or wrapped up in a roll.

CHAPTER 2

THE SIMPLEST DISH

People have eaten raw fish for thousands of years. People in China have eaten raw fish since 500 BCE. In the 700s CE, people in Japan began to eat fish raw as well.

LEARN MORE HERE!

Both sushi and sashimi are made from raw fish.
The two foods have some history in common.

They cut the fish into small strips. This

was the beginning of sashimi and **sushi**.

In the 700s, most of the fish was from rivers and lakes. Over the years, people began making sashimi from saltwater fish. They also started using **shellfish**.

Narezushi *is one of the earliest kinds of sushi. To make it, fish is pressed with rice and fermented for several months.*

Japan is a group of islands. Many people live on or near its coasts.

People **fermented** the fish so it would last longer. They added rice to the fish in the 1400s.

In Japan, people had easy access to fresh fish. They didn't need it to last as long. It could ferment less and still be safe to eat. People started eating it earlier in the process.

Soy sauce is often served in small bowls for dipping.

Sashimi took on its current form starting in the 1600s. By that time, **soy sauce** had become cheap and easy to buy. Soy sauce made it easier to eat the raw fish. People started dipping sashimi in it. They also added **wasabi**.

Wasabi is a bright-green paste made by grinding an herb.

Tuna is a common fish used in sashimi. It can be found all over the world.

For many years, sashimi was mainly eaten in Asia. Then, in the 1960s, people invented better refrigerators. Fresh fish could be delivered all over the world quickly. Sushi restaurants began opening in North America. These restaurants often served sashimi as well.

DID YOU KNOW?

The first sushi restaurant in the United States opened in 1966.

CHAPTER 3

IN THE KITCHEN

Sashimi is not cooked. So, making sashimi is all about knife work. Chefs start with a fresh, raw fish. They cut a fillet, or a strip of meat with no bones. Then they

TRY A RECIPE HERE!

Many sashimi chefs use yanagiba *knives. Their blades are long, thin, and very sharp.*

chop the fillet into small, thin pieces.

They stack these slices on plates.

Many types of fish and seafood can be used in sashimi. Tuna and salmon are popular choices. People may also use octopus or squid. Every fish has a different flavor. Chefs learn which cuts help each fish taste best.

DID YOU KNOW?

Many people think bluefin tuna is the best fish for sashimi. Just 1 pound (0.5 kg) of this rare fish can cost $40 to $200.

TUNA CUTS FOR SASHIMI

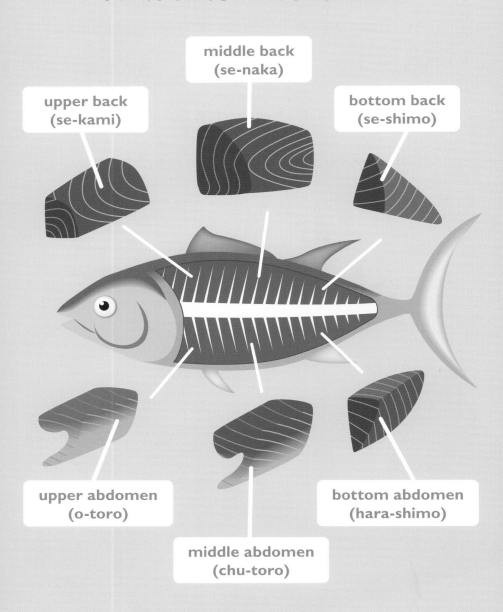

middle back
(se-naka)

upper back
(se-kami)

bottom back
(se-shimo)

upper abdomen
(o-toro)

bottom abdomen
(hara-shimo)

middle abdomen
(chu-toro)

The chef sometimes adds vegetables to the plate. These are usually cabbage or white turnips. Diners don't always eat these vegetables. But they make the

Sashimi is often served with lemon.

Chefs place each piece carefully to create beautiful patterns.

plate look nice. Sashimi is also served

with **wasabi** and **soy sauce**.

RECIPE CHECKLIST

INGREDIENTS

- 1 pound fillet of tuna
- 2 tablespoons wasabi paste
- soy sauce for dipping
- 1/2 cup grated cabbage
- 1/2 cup grated white turnip

Makes 4 servings

INSTRUCTIONS

1. Starting on the right side of the fillet, slice the fish into 0.4-inch- (1-cm) thick pieces.

2. Place a bed of cabbage and turnips on a serving plate.

3. Arrange the fish pieces in stacks on top of the vegetables.

4. Place a dime-sized dab of wasabi on a corner of the plate.

5. Serve with a small bowl of soy sauce.

CHAPTER 4

SASHIMI EVERYWHERE

People eat some foods made from raw fish at home. But for sashimi, people usually go to a restaurant. Sashimi chefs know to get the freshest fish. They only buy it from sellers they trust. Then they

COMPLETE AN ACTIVITY HERE!

prepare it carefully. That way, people are

less likely to get sick.

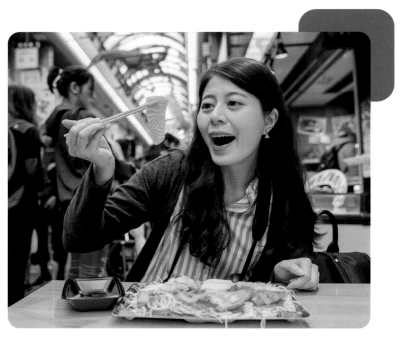

Many fish markets have restaurants where people can order fresh sashimi.

The Toyosu Market in Tokyo is the biggest fish market in the world. It has many shops and restaurants.

Restaurants often base their menus on what fish are available. Some restaurants even keep tanks of live fish.

These fish are grabbed from the tanks and used for sashimi that night.

Fugu is sliced much thinner than other sashimi meats.

FUGU

Fugu is a type of blowfish. It is poisonous to anything that tries to eat it, including humans. But some people can make it into sashimi. Chefs must get a special license to serve fugu. They go through years of training. They learn to cut around the poisonous parts. Even a small bit of poison can be deadly.

There is an **etiquette** to eating sashimi. People pour the amount of **soy sauce** they need in a bowl. Then they dab **wasabi** on the fish. They pick up the fish with chopsticks. Then they dip it in the soy sauce.

People eat one piece of sashimi at a time.

Chamchi hoe *is a style of tuna sashimi from Korea.*

MAKING CONNECTIONS

TEXT-TO-SELF

Would you want to become a sashimi chef?
Why or why not?

TEXT-TO-TEXT

Have you read other books about seafood?
How is sashimi similar to or different from the
foods mentioned in those books?

TEXT-TO-WORLD

People who live on islands often have access to
fresh fish. How else might the places people live
affect the kinds of foods they eat?

bacteria — tiny life-forms that can cause illness.

etiquette — a set of rules about how to behave.

ferment — to go through a process in which the sugars in food change into alcohol.

shellfish — a creature that lives underwater and has a shell.

soy sauce — a salty dipping sauce made from soybeans.

sushi — cold rice with vinegar rolled into shapes and paired with seafood and vegetables.

wasabi — a paste made from a green root with a strong taste.

INDEX

ONLINE RESOURCES

popbooksonline.com

Scan this code* and others like it while you read, or visit the website below to make this book pop!

popbooksonline.com/sashimi

*Scanning QR codes requires a web-enabled smart device with a QR code reader app and a camera.